T0282682

YOU BE THE
JUDGE

YOU BE THE
JUDGE

HE SAID, SHE SAID

Play by
A.M. Nesia

ARCHWAY
PUBLISHING

Archway Publishing books may be ordered through booksellers or by contacting:

Archway Publishing
1663 Liberty Drive
Bloomington, IN 47403
www.archwaypublishing.com
1 (888) 242-5904

ISBN: 978-1-4808-3323-4 (sc)
ISBN: 978-1-4808-3324-1 (e)

Library of Congress Control Number: 2016910172

Print information available on the last page.

Archway Publishing rev. date: 06/17/2016

CONTENTS

CHARACTERS

He

She

Woman

Eight extras (male and female).

PROLOGUE

Silence for the count of ten, nine, eight ... ... tick tock sound.

Her voice off stage begins.

In the darkness before you sleep ... .(wait counting 10,9,8 then)
what do you think about ... ... (wait counting 10,9,8 then)
what you did today ... ... (wait counting 10,9,8 then)
what you will do tomorrow ... .(wait counting 10,9,8 then)
what do you hope to ... ... (wait counting 10,9,8 then)

Female (spotlight light on her) sitting fore stage cramped barely fitting in a cardboard box one leg with knee bent, the other leg up resting against the wall side of box, her knee almost touching her face and her right hand danglingly off the stage.* She is dressed in a hospital gown and sleepers.

She: me - I think about how to accomplish the impossible ... ...
       (wait counting 10,9,8 then)

why because until something happens to you that in a moment changes who you are ... ... (wait counting 10,9,8 then) what you can do ... ... (wait counting 10,9,8 then)

because you have become fearless ... ... (wait counting 10,9,8 then)

She kicks the wall of the box, freeing herself from the box.

Entire stage lights up but not her. She disappears below through a hided door.

Mary Poppin's music begins to play and the stage is lit up with flickering streams of fuschia pink.**

The music is lowered so her voice can be clearly heard and lighting again back on her.

Standing facing fore stage left looking wistfully upward toward the right.

She: Oh so happy was I?! ... .(wait counting 10,9,8 then)

Single and independent then in a moment it changed for the better, for the worse ... ... (wait counting 10,9,8 then)

Oh - you decide, it has become too exhausting for me now as time goes on ... ... (wait counting 10,9,8 then) cuckoo sounds

all I know is I fear NOTHING ... ... (wait counting 10,9,8 then)

I try to understand but end up thinking who cares really … … .

(wait counting 10,9,8 then)

really who cares? … … … (wait counting 10,9,8 then)

will you? … … … .(wait counting 10,9,8 then)

do YOU? … … … .(wait counting 10,9,8 then)

Stage goes black.

Yodelling music for thirty seconds.

The cyclorama is a beautiful Alps scene and the phrase

"everything is beautiful and nothing hurts"

is dropped down from above in a Tracy Emin type scroll in white neon. A red leather chair with a clear glass ashtray with an orange base resting on arm of the chair is on the left stage.

A cuckoo clock is spinning backwards and suddenly starts to cuckoo … …

She walks on stage cuckoo stops. She is smoking and carrying a gavel in the other hand. She is wearing a Boss high neckline short sleeve blue dress and three inch navy pumps. She begins to walk counterclockwise around stage. Swinging the gavel and smoking between lines.

She: Please try if you do care … .to think about it … …

what he said, she said … …

his truth? … … (wait counting 10,9,8 then) tick sound

her truth? … … (wait counting 10,9,8 then) (takes a drag)

what is right? … .(wait counting 10,9,8 then) tock sound

what is wrong? … … (wait counting 10,9,8 then) (takes a drag)

what is good? … .(wait counting 10,9,8 then) tick sound

what is bad? … .(wait counting 10,9,8 then) (takes a drag)

who lies? … … (wait counting 10,9,8 then) tock sound

who tells the truth? … … (wait counting 10,9,8 then) (takes a drag)

who is innocent? … … (wait counting 10,9,8 then) tick sound

how does your past and present even your future determine what you think? … … (wait counting 10,9,8 then) tock sound

now that you are confronted with this story will it change you? … … (wait counting 10,9,8 then) tick sound

do you? will you? DOUBT?? … … .(wait counting 10,9,8 then) (takes a drag)

[A bunch of female mouths appear on the cyclorama opening and closing. The top row of teeth are all cap and white, the bottom row are discolored and small with gaps between.]

Regardless of the speculation and gossip ... .

[She stops walking, takes a drag and changes from walking counterclockwise to clockwise.]

It comes down to PS&M not PMS ... .(wait counting 10,9,8 then) (takes a drag)

POWER SEX AND MONEY

You ... ... YOU be the judge.

[She takes along drag and another.]

She: POWER SEX AND MONEY (gently puts out the cigarette slowly while saying it.)

You be the judge. (She takes the gavel and smashes the ashtray.)

The cyclorama lights up with scattered orange and clear glass the pieces come together and form an edelweiss flower in orange. Lights down on the stage.

Spotlight is on her as she gets up out of the chair and walks off with her back to the audience.

ACT I
Winter

Yodeling music for thirty seconds.

Cyclorama is a beautiful Alps scene.

Also video screen on left stage simply states " he said." And video screen on the right stage simply states " she said."

Text across the cyclorama

He: My brother suggests a famous spa. Let's meet at the station 3pm.
She: Great.
He: See you there

After using the spa, they are lounging on two lounge chairs positioned to be looking at the Alps at an oblique angle. There is a woman in her fifties, in a robe sitting to her right reading a book.

He lifts his towel exposing himself, and the fact he likes blue pills.

He: Lift up yours
She: Huh?

She turns and looks at the woman engrossed in her book. And she looks back at him.

He gets up and walks away. He comes back and leads her the sunbed area where he begins to pleasure himself.

He: Lie on the sunbed.

Looks like a casket and not comfortable looking but she gets in it ... ... He is sitting on a stool beside her.

Lights out.

She: What are you doing that hurts?
He: All the girls like it.
She: Not this one.

Total Blackout ... ... (wait 10, 9, 8 ... ... then) tick tock sound

Lights back on and they are both standing in a same locker room. He is dressed. However; she is not.

Light focuses on her and fades on him.

Her: Why I am in the changing room getting changed and focusing on his big oversized navy coat - his Dad's?! How did he get dressed so fast? And I am still in a towel? What happened? ... .

Lights out.

Cuckoo sounds.

ACT 2
Summer

City streets and sounds on cyclorama.

Texts run across the stage above .... .

He: Would like to come over for a drink this afternoon?
She: Sure
He: Great see you 5ish
She: k see you later

Small two bedroom walkup facing the back of the building on the fifth floor. There are two windows and on the left is an open kitchen with a L-shaped counter that has couple of bar stools. On the right of apartment; there is a small living room with built in bookshelf next to the window on the right, hardly anything on it, a black pseudo Eames chair, small wood coffee table and a small black vinyl leather couch.

He is in a white teeshirt and jeans, barefoot. He is standing in the kitchen back to audience opening the wine and turns around to pour it. He takes something from the cupboard and drops it in the glass on the counter. He is holding his glass in his left hand.

He: Hello.
She: Hello.
He: Welcome ... have a seat at the bar. Would you like a glass of wine?
She: Yes thanks.
He: Have some chips.

7

Their voices lower; they smile and chat for a minute sitting at the kitchen counter.

Lights lower.

He: Would you like to check out the roof?
She: Mmm sure (nodding her head)
He: Right this way be careful the stairs aren't that safe.

Once up the stairs.

He: This is it - nice right?!

Both are looking at the major hotel construction site going up next door.

She: Nice view and nice to be able to be outside when the weather is so perfect.
He: Yeah, it is great. My brother was here the last week and we hung out here. He was a little high and try to climb that wall.

He glances over and sees people out on the neighboring roof.

He: Why don't we go back inside? (sheepishly)

Back inside, he sits on a chair and she stands in front of him.

He: Let's see what we have here.

He undoes her white halter top dress with flower print.

She says nothing, does nothing. He leads her to the bedroom.

She runs out goes to kitchen sink and gets a glass of water. She puts it down next to bed. She gets on bed.

She: Play nice.
He: I want to rape you … … (wait 10, 9, 8 … .then) tick tock sound

Lights go out.

Next, she is writing on a small piece of notepad paper.

Spotlight on her.

She: How did I get here? How am I already dressed? Why am I so annoyed? What happened? I got up to get a glass of water and then what?

Light up on stage. He is standing in kitchen in front of sink and she is sitting on a bar stool, writing furiously.

She: Ok … … so let's see either you aren't interested one or have a girlfriend two or I don't know three (writing on the notepad). Help me out here.

He standing at the fridge takes a newspaper article off the fridge door.

He: Did you give this to me?

She: Huh? No and are you going to answer this?

He: Ok, no then it isn't important. I'll throw it away.

He digging in a kitchen drawer, next to the fridge.

He: Have this I bought it in DR for you.

She: Ah … thanks. (looking at him puzzled)

She looks and sees a silver shoe/ umbrella/ bag (not quite sure) on the floor in partly opened closet … … …

ACT 3
Winter

Backstage street scene

He: I am at a hotel just like the one in photo. You should come.

She: Ok - let me check flights.

He: You realize there is a blizzard on the way you might get stuck?

Seconds later ... ...

She: No problem booked.

Sitting at the hotel bar.

He: So Mary Poppins is playing across the street we could see that. Also, the concierge recommends a nice Italian restaurant, 5 minutes away.

She: Sounds great.

A little later after chatting and talking with the woman behind bar.

He: We can catch a taxi.

She: Let's walk.

He: It is more than a mile!

She: And?? It is snowing out. It is beautiful.

After dinner, they are standing outside the restaurant. He looks at his watch.

He: Looks like we won't make a show. How about a strip club?

She: I have never been. Ok?

Inside the club, basically, a sports bar with a few topless girls with pasties.

He: Guys in here are all probably from the steel convention.
She: Oh, there is another couple. (with a sound of relief)

The other couple seems to be enjoying themselves laughing; the woman is getting the lap dance.

He: Odd all the girls are white?
She: What? Ah.. .... this is the Midwest.
He: They are missing light brown girls.
She: Huh? (Looks away in disbelief)

Now back in the boutique hotel room; a very small room for two with one queen size bed. There is a mirrored wall made to look stylish with golden cracks throughout, flat screen tv on top of mini fridge, a leather chair and Herman chair at the long desk. She sits on the bed. She can puts her bag down.

He: I sleep naked.
She: Ok, so do I.

Before she knows it, he is naked standing in front of her.

She: Nice.

Said sarcastically as she unzips her boots and takes them off .... .

He walks to bathroom asking would you like to split a drink?

She: Sure

Spotlight on her rest of stage dims.

She: Who splits a drink?

He hands her a drink.

He: Proust
She: Proust

She drinks it and continues to undress. He is on bed.

He: My shoulder is bothering me.
She: Oh ... ...
He: Could you give me a massage?

Already sitting up expecting one with his back to her, she goes and sits behind him. Lights go dark and spotlight goes on her.

She: Why I am giving him the massage? Didn't he say once that he is good at giving massages?

Lights back on.

She: Nah, I am going to sleep.

She gets under the covers and he flings them back off. And he looks at her and starts to pleasure himself. Then without saying anything is sitting over her with one leg between her legs.

She hears a man clearing his throat through the thin hotel wall.

Lights go out ... ... (10, 9, 8 ... ... .then) tick tock sound

Lights on her for a split second and then again for a split second. The bed is up in the air! Her head is off the end of bed and he is over her, leaning back with one arm up over his head as if in a moment of triumph.

Lights on ... ... (10, 9, 8.. ... then)

He lying on bed facing her, she is lying on her side facing him, under the covers.

He: I am going to sleep. Nite.
She: Nite.

Lights out. Spotlight on her.

She: Why am under the covers???

Lights out ... ... (10, 9, 8 ... .then)

16

She: Morning. Coffee?

He: There isn't any.

She: Room service?

He: Ok

She calls room service.

He: How am I going to explain two on my bill?

Lights go out ... ... Spotlight on her.

She: He can't be serious. We go out and come back, get naked and we don't fool around and now this comment. Huh? What? What happened?

She ignores him and turns on tv. CNBC is covering Davos Economic forum live.

He: Hey look at this ... .

She disappears into the bathroom puts on some makeup. He follows and starts brushing his teeth. She writes something on the mirror and erases it.

He walks out of bathroom. She follows and goes to get her bag.

He goes to closet and pulls out a set of lingerie with an animal print.

He: Next time, will you where this?

Lights out ... ... Spotlight on her.

She: Ok huh? What is he talking about? Am in Vegas? What
        happened? And is there lingerie in every closet in this hotel?
        So many questions? I am totally confused. Why?

Lights on

She: Let's go ... ...

ACT 4
Fall

Sitting outside at a cafe, they are having a drink. She is taking the stirrer and mashing her lime in her gin and tonic.

Text arrives on her her phone. It states late start at 10am. She texts back k thx. Text comes back k.

She: Ok late start tomorrow you want to walk. I'll show you a cool place.
He: Yeah ok.

They walk making a bet on whether a restaurant they pass is owned by so and so.

They arrive at a beauiful place, a lounge/restaurant; a bunch of people are sitted talking in hushed tones, Leonard Cohen music playing so softly you can barely hear it. She walks over to the fireplace and puts out her hands to warm them.

She: I love this place. It is actually private. (Whispering in his ear)
She: Happy my hands are warm didn't realize I was so cold.
He: You know I have a fireplace.
She: You do? Really?
He: You want to see.
She: Yes
He: Ok let's go.

They are inside a sparsely furnished apt with a fireplace.

He: I am going to change. You want to come up and see the terrace.

They go upstairs. He tries on one of the new tee-shirts, he purchased while they were out earlier that says " Nice" and the other "Cool."

She: Nice terrace must be great to have the doors open at night.
He: Yes and no. One night had two Eastern Europeans girls somehow show up on it.

He is inside changing shirts. She is outside on terrace.

He: Too small right?
She: Yes, I can stop by there tomorrow and change them for you.

They go back downstairs.

He: I will make drinks. You want to start a fire.
She: Ok

Both begin their tasks he steps into four by four foot kitchen. He comes back in room. She has taken off shoes and just finished starting the fire. He hands her a drink.

He: Salud!
She: Cheers.

He: Want to see some pictures from the art opening.
She: Sure

They are both sitting on the floor.

He: That is my Mom.

She: Oh Did she actually like the art?

He: Yes, she thought it was interesting.

On cyclorama, a video plays of an opening which would be held two years later, in same venue as the art opening. The video was filmed by him on her iphone.

He: Take off your underwear.

She takes off her underwear and he is once again is pleasuring himself.

She goes to bathroom comes back and notices the fire needs some help as she didn't put enough smaller logs to get it really going. She bends down to put in a few smaller logs and then bends down on her hands and knees and starts to blow on the fire. He has gotten up and is now behind her. He picks up the fire poker positioning it right behind her as close as he can get it to her.

Lights go out ... ...

Spot light on her face.

She: What is that???? What is he doing????

Lights out.

His voice plays overhead " sorry, sorry, sorry ... ... ", over and over again. This voice is from a video of his shoe at art opening two years later, taken apparently?! by accident just after the video that was just played on the cyclorama.

Lights on ... ...

He has gotten up sitting on sofa. She approaches him and he leaps across the room sits on the back of a chair turns on the tv.

He: You want to watch porn.
She: No
He: What do you want to watch?
She: 30Rock

Lights go out ... ...(10, 9, 8 ... ... then) tick tock sound

Spotlight on her. She has the shopping bag in hand.

She: Ok what just happened? I must be the stupidest person on
        the planet. Why did I agreed to exchange these tee-shirts?

(She holds up bag looking at it as if it is some foreign object.)

She: I was always taught to kill them with kindest. But what just
        happened? What just happened?

ACT 5
Summer

Stage goes black.

Light goes to female sitting forestage cross legged on a bigger cardboard box in hospital gown and slippers smoking no ashtray but flicks the ashes directly onto the stage floor.

Upstage the dancers (women) in nude costumes begin to building boxes behind her with the open end to the audience and disappear offstage.

She: All he said she said ... (wait 10, 9, 8 then)

So how does it feel to be able to judge the truth? (Staring in the audience) ... ... (wait 10, 9, 8,7, 6, 5, 4, 3, 2,1 ... ...)

No one was hurt so it doesn't count right? The detective said I should consider myself lucky.

Strips off gown revealing her navy dress.

Slips out of hospital slippers into high heels.

A glass of champagne, Vueve Clicquot, descends from above as if from heaven.

She: À votre sante! She takes it sips slowly while ... ...

Fore stage right, there is a pitcher of water and two empty glasses on the dinner table and bouquet of old flowers that should have been thrown out two days ago, petals falling off and water has turned. The woman who has long curly hair with glasses is sitting cross legged, wearing a short sleeve white top and blue and white batik pants; her thin black bra strap is off her shoulder but she doesn't notice. She is staring at the flowers as if paralyzed.

He walks in with two small dogs; one hops in into woman's lap. He is wearing long workout shorts, tee shirt and baseball cap. And the other dog hops onto a pseudo black Eames chair covered with a navy blanket just for the dog. He grabs a beer from fridge.

He: Want one?
Woman: Yes

He opens the beer, hands it to the woman and grabs another for himself. He sits at table and takes a cigarette from the pack starts fiddling with a cigarette. He gets up and goes to window and lights it up.

He: I don't know what to do. (He takes a long drag and
         another.)
Woman: I told you she was crazy.

He looks out the window.

Spotlight goes to her in dress, holding a candle. The woman is putting her hair up in a tight bun on top of her head and slips into short sleeve summer dress.

She: I don't care if he****** on the subway platform. What type
         of person says that?

She blows out the candle.

The woman pours two glasses of water, handing one to him.

Woman: I called 9II ... ... (wait 10, 9, 8 then) ... ... she is
         going to county jail ... ... Next time, we see her on
         the block ... ... (wait 10, 9, 8 then) we will in her
         face ... ...

He: Next time, we see her on the block ... ... (wait 10,
         9, 8 then) we will in her face ... ...

He takes his phone out of his pocket and gives it to her and he
takes his glass of water and throws it, almost splashing it in the
audience.

The woman takes her phone out of her pocket and gives it to him
and the woman takes her glass of water and throws it, almost
splashing it in the audience.

He takes a drag and hands the cigarette to her.

Woman: You video me doing that and we will see the ******
         ****** in court.

She takes a drag and flicks it out the window. She grabs his face with both hands and kisses him.

Woman: For better … … .(wait 10, 9, 8 then) for worse.

She turns around and walks back to table. Meanwhile, he has taken a tiny piece of something out of his pocket. A piece of glass, orange on one side he rolls it slowly in his fingers loooking at it.

Cyclorama lights up with broken orange glass and suddenly goes out.

She picks up both beers walks over to him as he tosses it out the window. She sees him do it.

Woman: What was that?
He: Fernweh …
Woman: Huh?!
He: Cheers!
Woman: Cheers

Lights out on the couple.

Spotlight on her.

She: Now the truth is they said? she said? … … (wait 10, 9, 8 … … .then)
She: Il faut que j'aille.

The dancers then turn all the boxes and around which have written in helvetica typeset.

Not just a box but a voice with a box

She walks off stage with her back to the audience.

Lights go out … … … (wait 10,9, 8 and then) tick tock sound.

Three neon signs come down against the Alps scene with five innocent children's faces on cyclorama: three Heidi looking girls with braided pigtails and bangs, and one boy.

One red: Heimweh

One white: "everything is beautiful and nothing hurts"

One blue: Fernweh

tick tock sound. cuckoo sounds once.

A man with his hair slicked back dressed in all white; unclear if it is an officer, orderly, angel, escort, colleague, boyfriend or spouse on her left opens an umbrella puts his arm around her. Spotlight goes from being on both of them to just on her, his arm is no longer around her shoulder and it begins to rain upstage. It changes from rainwater to raining money on the umbrella.

EPILOGUE

The video on left and right stage changes from " he said " to " they said."

Donner sa langue au chat.

Character is a man's fate.

NOTES

Heimweh: German for homesickness. Originated in German for psychosomatic disorder was first treated in 1678 by the Swiss Physician Johannes Hoferus, who also gave it the Greek name " nostalgia."

Fernweh: German for a desire to be in faraway places. Like Heimweh has a melancholy twinge.

German words chosen from a Voyages article by T. Cole in NY TIMES Sept 2015 about his stay as writer-in-residence in Zurich.

Stage lightening reference STORMAE concert MSG and videos.

* Time out magazine Sept 30 2015 Field Farm photo p60.
** Styled on fushia pink metallic pom poms reflecting sunlight.